Superfun

DOG Crafts

Toby's Toys

All Crafts
in This Book Were
DOG TESTED AND
DOG APPROVED

Jane Yates

Gareth Stevens
PUBLISHING

Published in 2019 by Gareth Stevens,
an Imprint of Rosen Publishing
29 East 21st Street, New York, NY 10010

Developed and produced for Rosen by BlueAppleWorks Inc.

Creative Director: Melissa McClellan
Managing Editor for BlueAppleWorks: Melissa McClellan
Designer: T.J. Choleva
Photo Research: Jane Reid
Editor: Marcia Abramson

Craft Artisans: Jane Yates (p. 8, 10, 12, 14,16, 18, 20, 22, 24, 26, 28)

Photo Credits: © cover center, p. 15 Dorottya Mathe/Shutterstock.com; cover top left Austen Photography; cover top right Austen Photography; cover middle rightAusten Photography; cover bottom right mariait/Shutterstock.com; Paw print Dreamzdesigners/Shutterstock.com; p. 4 left Africa Studio/Shutterstock.com; p 4 top right Martin Valigursky/Dreamstime; p. 4 top right middle Melle V/Shutterstock.com; p. 4 bottom right middle ESB Professiona/Shutterstock.com; p. 4 bottom right MJTH/Shutterstock.com; p. 5 top left Mila Atkovska/Dreamstime; p. 5 middle left Paologozzi/Dreamstime; p. 5 bottom left, 27 Cynoclub/Dreamstime; p. 5 top right Graphicphoto/Dreamstime; p. 5 bottom right Ksenia Raykova/ Dreamstime; p. 6, 9 Erik Lam/Shutterstock.com; p. 8 WilleeCole Photography/Shutterstock.com; p. 11 sonya etchison/Shutterstock.com; p. 13 Eric Isselee/Shutterstock.com; p. 17 Elena Elisseeva/Shutterstock.com; p. 18 Austen Photography; p. 23, 25 cynoclub/Shutterstock.com; p. 28 Austen Photography; p. 29 Austen Photography; p. 32 left Csanad Kiss/Shutterstock.com; p. 32 right Susan Schmitz/Shutterstock.com; back cover left to right:WilleeCole Photography/Shutterstock.com; Austen Photography; cynoclub/Shutterstock.com; Cynoclub/Dreamstime; All craft photography Austen Photography

Cataloging-in-Publication-Data
Names: Yates, Jane.
Title: Superfun dog crafts / Jane Yates.
Description: New York : Gareth Stevens Publishing, 2019. | Series: Get crafty with pets! | Includes glossary and index.
Identifiers: LCCN ISBN 9781538226155 (pbk.) | ISBN 9781538226148 (library bound) | ISBN 9781538226162 (6 pack)
Subjects: LCSH: Handicraft--Juvenile literature. | Dogs--Juvenile literature. | Dogs in art--Juvenile literature. | Pets--Juvenile literature. | Pet supplies--Juvenile literature.
Classification: LCC TT160.Y38 2019 | DDC 745.59--dc23

Manufactured in the United States of America

CPSIA Compliance Information: Batch #CS18GS For Further Information contact: Rosen Publishing, New York, New York at 1-800-237-9932

Linus

Good Dog!

Contents

TOBY's Cookies

Dogs as Pets

Our furry four-legged companions evolved from wolves into our best friends. Scientists believe wolves were first attracted to human camps to scavenge for leftover food. Over time, some wolves started traveling with people.

Now, there are many breeds of dogs around the world. They have different personalities, different purposes, and come in many different sizes. However, they all have one thing in common—they're our best friends. Dogs make us happy, love us back, are great company, are entertaining, are great protectors, and give the best welcome home!

Dogs are loyal friends and companions. They want to belong to a pack, whether it's made up of dogs or humans.

DOGS MAKE US HAPPY

DOGS LOVE US BACK

DOGS GIVE THE BEST WELCOME HOME

Dog Photography

You might want to take pictures of your pet dog and use them for some craft projects. Read the tips below and try taking pictures of dogs.

Make sure your pet feels comfortable. Instead of bringing your dog to you, go to where your dog likes to be. Get down on the ground to take photos on the animal's level—don't take all the photos from above. It's best to take the photos outside or near a window. Use treats and your pet's favorite toys to reward your dog. Take lots of pictures from different angles.

EYE LEVEL

CLOSE-UP

HIGH ANGLE

ACTION

LOW ANGLE

Photo Tip

Have someone stand beside you with a treat or squeaky toy to get the dog to look at the camera.

Techniques

These projects are great for dog lovers whether you have a dog or hope to have a dog in the future (make and save the toys in a dog hope chest), or to give as gifts to someone you know who has a dog. Most of the materials in this book can be easily found. You may have some of them already. Others can be purchased at craft or dollar stores. Use the following techniques to create your crafts.

PAPER-MACHE GLUE

> Add equal amounts of white glue and water in a bowl. Mix the glue and water together with a spoon. If you have leftover glue, put it in a container with a lid and use it later. (An empty yogurt container works well.)

THREADING A NEEDLE

> Use a **tapestry** needle for working with yarn and embroidery thread.

> Wet one end of the thread in your mouth. Poke it through the needle opening. Pull some of the thread through until you have an even amount and make a double knot.

> For yarn, fold a piece of yarn over, then push the fold through the opening. This is easier than using a single thread.

Put the thread through the loop.

Fold the yarn, then feed it through the loop.

A NOTE ABOUT MEASUREMENTS

Measurements are given in U.S. form with metric in parentheses. For fractions like ¼ inch, a less-than-whole metric number is given to make it easier to measure.

Running Stitch

> Use a running stitch to sew one piece of material to another piece.

> Thread a needle, then tie a knot at the other end.

> Place the needle and knotted thread underneath the two pieces of material. Weave the thread in and out through both layers of material.

> Continue stitching until finished.

> When you are done sewing, tie a knot on the back of the material to hold the stitches in place.

Using Patterns

> Patterns help you cut out exact shapes when crafting.

> Use tape to attach the pattern to the cloth or paper before you start cutting.

> When cutting out a shape, cut around the shape first, then make smaller cuts.

> When cutting with scissors, move the piece of material instead of the scissors.

> Make sure you keep your fingers out of the way while cutting. Ask an adult for help if needed.

Trace the pattern.

Cut the pattern out.

Attach the pattern to the material.

Cut the material along the pattern lines.

Tip

If your dog starts to destroy a toy, take it away from your pet.

Be Prepared

> Read through the instructions and make sure you have all the materials you need.

> Clean up when you are finished making your crafts. Put away your supplies for next time.

Be Safe

> Ask for help when you need it.

> Ask for permission to borrow tools.

> Be careful when using scissors and needles.

Dog Bed

Make a cute dog bed from an old sweater.

Tools & Materials:

✔ Sweater
✔ Safety pins
✔ Yarn
✔ Tapestry needle
✔ Scissors
✔ Stuffing

1. Find a sweater bigger than your dog. (A thrift store is a good place to look if you don't have one.) Turn the sweater inside out.

2. Fold the sweater opening over and use safety pins to hold it in place. Thread the yarn onto the tapestry needle. (Use a color that matches your sweater. The illustration uses a non-matching color so that the yarn is visible.) Start sewing with the running stitch.

3. Leave an opening for the stuffing. Stitch back to where you started so that you have a double row of stitches. Tie a knot and trim the yarn.

4. Stitch the end of both sleeves closed using two rows of running stitch.

5. Turn your sweater **right side** out. Using stuffing, stuff the inside through the opening at the bottom of the sweater. Fill the arms first and then the rest of the sweater.

6. Pull the arms together and stitch together. Stitch the back corners of the sweater to the arms, with a few stitches for each corner. Stitch the arms to the sides of the sweater in the middle on each side.

2 Sew

Secure with safety pins

3

Leave opening

4

Sew

Dogs sleep a lot! Adult dogs sleep from 12 to 14 hours a day depending on their age, how active they are, and size. Large breed dogs might spend up to 18 hours a day sleeping! Don't poke a sleeping dog. If you want to wake a dog, call it or make a sound from the other side of the room.

5

Fill with stuffing

6

Sew

Treat Jar

Make a treat jar to store dog biscuits! It can be for your own dog or a gift for a special dog you know.

Tools & Materials:

✔ Mason jar
✔ Glue
✔ Small plastic dog
✔ Paint (regular and puffy)
✔ Paintbrush

1 Find a clean mason jar that you can use for your treat jar.

2 Remove the lid. Take the lid apart. Put glue along the bottom edge of the center piece.

3 Place it into the rim and leave to dry.

4 Glue the plastic dog to the top of the lid.

5 Paint a label on the jar with puffy paint.

6 Paint the lid and dog. Leave to dry.

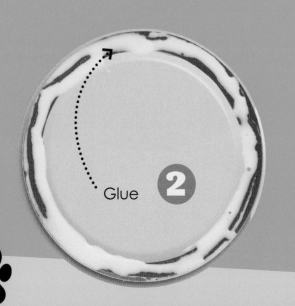

Glue 2

3 Place into rim, glue side down

4

Glue

Another IDEA!

Make a label for your jar. Use a computer or hand-draw a label. Cut it out in a circle shape. Cut out another circle from cardboard. Glue them together. Punch a hole and use a piece of string to tie it to the jar.

TOBY'S Cookies

Did You Know?

Just like we do, dogs love treats. And just like us, dogs sometimes get too many calories from their treats, even though your dog would tell you there is no such thing as too many treats. Be careful to not give your dog too many!

5

Paint

MAX'S TREATS

6

Paint

11

Doggy Doorbell

Make a cute doggy doorbell so your dog can let you know when it needs to go outside.

Tools & Materials:
- ✔ Fleece (an old scarf or pajamas)
- ✔ Scissors and ruler
- ✔ Paper, pencil, and tape
- ✔ Felt
- ✔ Metal rings
- ✔ Tapestry needle and thread
- ✔ Large jingle bells

1. Cut a piece of fleece 4 inches (10 cm) wide and 24 inches (61 cm) long. Trace the circle **template** from page 30 onto paper and cut out. Tape to the fleece 2 inches (5 cm) from the top and centered.

2. Cut the circle out. Cut a slit at the bottom of the circle.

3. Cut out three small squares of felt. Slip two bells on each of the metal rings.

4. Cut a long piece of thread. Pull the thread through the needle until it is centered. Tie a knot with both loose ends. Place a felt square under the first spot to attach bells. Pull the needle through both the felt and the fleece. (The felt will make a more secure binding.)

5. While holding the ring with bells over the spot, sew over and under the ring, until the ring feels securely attached (about 20 times). Tie off the thread.

6. Repeat with the other two rings of bells.

7. Hang the bells over the door handle of the door where your dog goes out. Ring it every time you go out and your dog will soon learn to ring the bells when it needs to go out.

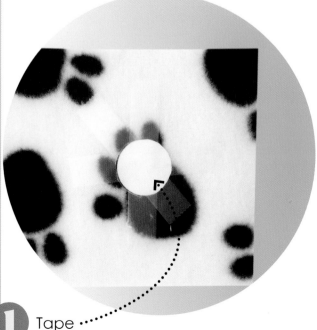

1. Tape

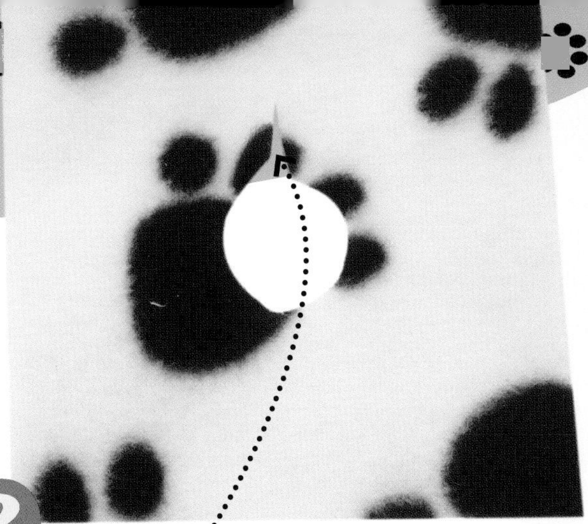

2

Cut slit

3

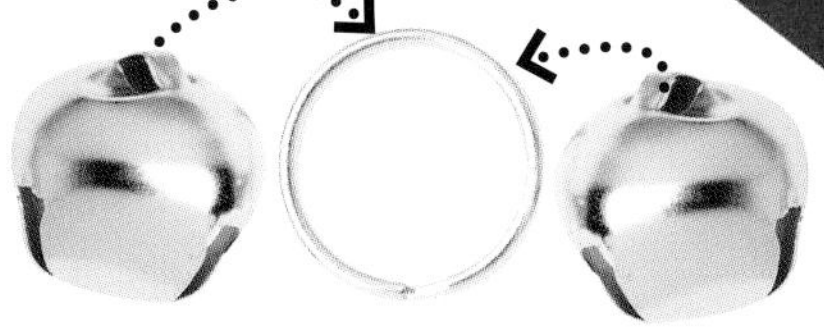

Slip on ring

Cut

4 Sew

5 Sew

Another IDEA!

Make your doggy doorbell with an old leash. Use the handle of the leash to hang on the door. Cut the leash to 24 inches (61 cm) long. Sew the bells onto the leash.

Did You Know?

The smartest dog breeds are border collie, golden retriever, poodle, and German shepherd. Other breeds may be smart, too, just not as eager to please people. Dogs recognize words and many dogs understand about 200 words. One smart border collie named Chaser learned over 1,000 words. Dogs do best with words for an object or action, such as "treat" and "walk."

Soft Bone

Make an adorable soft bone toy for your dog.

Tools & Materials:

✔ Paper and pencil
✔ Scissors
✔ Tape
✔ Fleece and/or flannel
✔ Safety pins
✔ Ruler
✔ Stuffing
✔ Embroidery thread
✔ Tapestry needle

1 Trace the bone template on page 30 onto paper and cut out. Tape the paper to a piece of fleece. Cut the bone shape out. Repeat with another piece of material but this time turn the pattern over before taping.

2 Place the two bones with the right sides together (this means the patterns will be on the inside).

9 Use safety pins to pin the bones together. Sew ¼ inch (.6 cm) from the edge around the bone. Leave an opening for the stuffing.

4 Using scissors, carefully make little snips around the edge of the bone. This will help your bone keep a nice shape. Turn the bone right side out.

5 Fill with stuffing.

6 Stitch the opening closed.

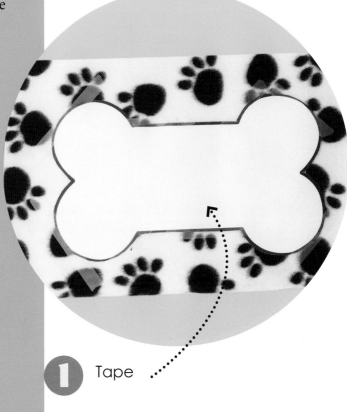

1 Tape

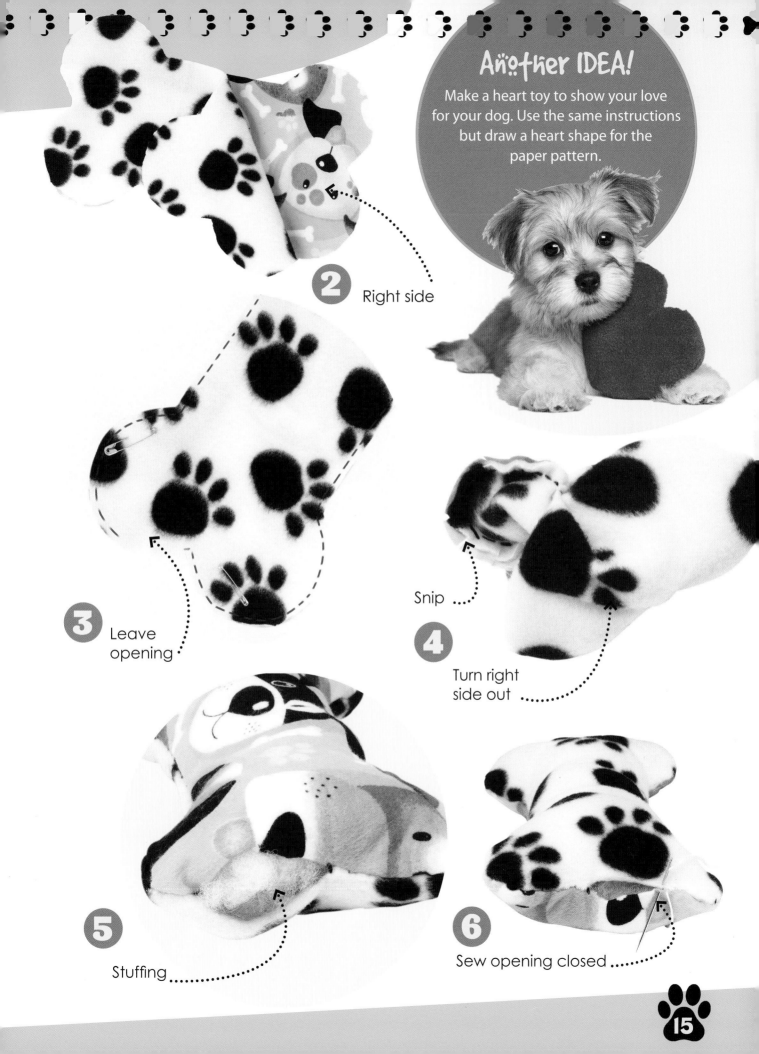

Another IDEA!

Make a heart toy to show your love for your dog. Use the same instructions but draw a heart shape for the paper pattern.

2 Right side

3 Leave opening

4 Snip

Turn right side out

5 Stuffing

6 Sew opening closed

Water Bottle Toy

For the dog who loves water bottles.

Tools & Materials:

✔ Fleece fabric (new or reused from an old blanket, sweater, or scarf)
✔ Scissors
✔ Old jeans
✔ Small water bottles
✔ Markers (optional)

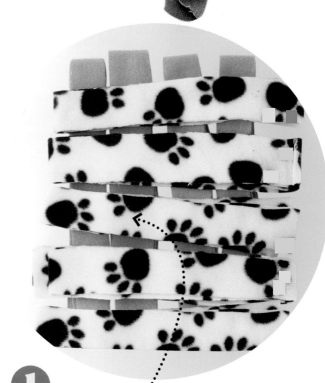

1. Cut nine strips of fleece about 1½ inches (4 cm) wide. (They don't need to be all exactly the same width.) Shown length is 60 inches (152 cm), but you can use shorter strips if your fleece is not that long.

2. Cut one leg from an old pair of jeans. Cut the hem off the bottom.

3. Tie three fleece strips around one end of the jean leg. Wrap the strips around and tie again and make a knot.

4. Place one of the water bottles into the jean opening. Tie three strips around the jeans to keep the bottle in place. Wrap the strips around and tie again and make a knot. Place the other water bottle into the jean leg. Tie three strips around the end of the jeans. Wrap the strips around and tie again and make a knot.

5. At one end separate the fleece into two sets of three strips. Braid the first set of three. Near the end make a knot. Repeat for each set of three fleece strips.

1. Cut strips

2

Cut

Another IDEA!

Cut the end off the other leg of the jeans. Tie a knot in the middle and you have an instant toy for your dog!

3

Tie three strips

4

Water bottle

5

Braid

17

Dog Frame

Make a special frame for your favorite dog photo.

Tools & Materials:

✔ Paper, pencil, and scissors
✔ Tape (clear and masking)
✔ Corrugated cardboard
✔ Paint and brush
✔ Glue
✔ Photo

Linus

Good Dog!

1. Trace the template of the bones on page 30 onto a piece of paper twice. Cut the pieces out.

2. Tape the pattern pieces to a piece of cardboard. Cut the cardboard pieces out and remove the pattern.

3. Paint the cardboard pieces. Leave to dry.

4. Lay the pieces out in a square shape. The two bone shapes go on top. Glue the bone shapes to the bottom pieces.

5. Turn the frame over. Cut a piece of cardboard slightly bigger than your photo. Tape your photo to the cardboard. Turn the cardboard over and tape it to the back of the bone frame.

6. Cut a small triangle of cardboard out. Tape it to the back of the frame to make an easel to hold the frame up.

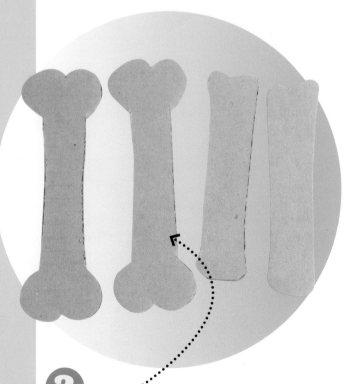

2 Cut

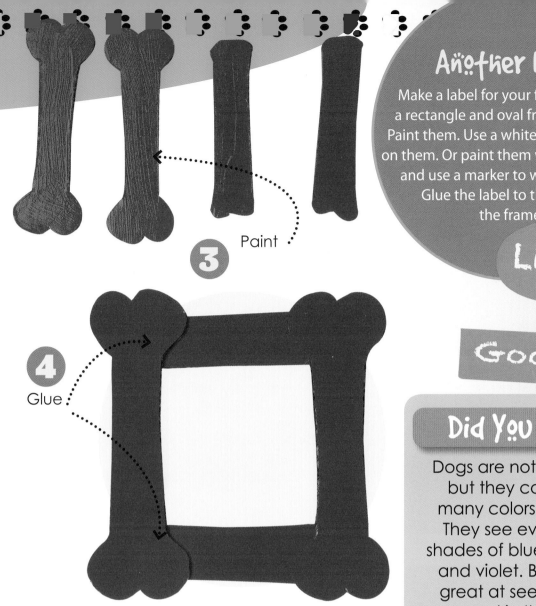

3 Paint

Another IDEA!

Make a label for your frame. Cut out a rectangle and oval from cardboard. Paint them. Use a white crayon to write on them. Or paint them with a light color and use a marker to write on them. Glue the label to the front of the frame.

Linus

4 Glue

Good Dog!

Did You Know?

Dogs are not color-blind, but they can't see as many colors as people. They see everything in shades of blue and yellow and violet. But they are great at seeing motion and in the dark.

5 Tape

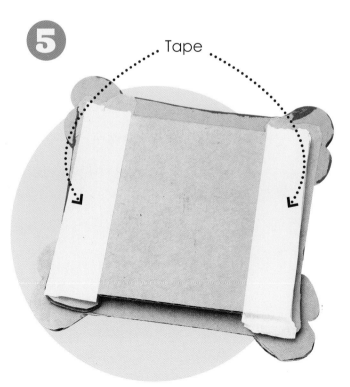

6

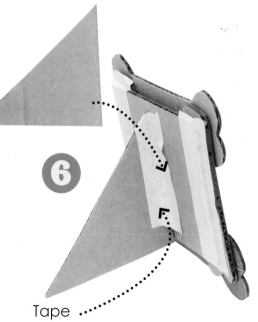

Tape

19

Pom-Pom Puppy

Make an adorable pom-pom puppy.

Tools & Materials:
- ✔ Bulky yarn
- ✔ Scissors
- ✔ Felt (4 colors)
- ✔ Glue
- ✔ Googly eyes
- ✔ Ruler

1. Make a large and small pom-pom using the instructions on page 31.

2. Cut two ear shapes from one color of felt. Cut a nose shape. Cut a tongue from pink felt. (There are patterns on page 31.) Cut a narrow strip for a collar from another color of felt.

3. Use scissors to trim the smaller pom-pom to look like a dog head with a nose. Cut small amounts until you are happy with the shape.

4. Glue the googly eyes above the nose. Glue the ears to the side. Glue the tongue below the nose.

5. Make three chains: one for the tail, one for the front legs, and one for the back legs. Cut a 6-inch (15 cm) piece of yarn. Fold it in half. Make a knot. Repeat making knots until you have a chain. Repeat two more times. Cut three small pieces of yarn. Tie to the middle of two chains. Tie the other to the end of a chain.

6. Tie the three chains to the large pom-pom, making legs and a tail. Fluff the pom-pom.

7. Tie the two pom-poms together. Glue the felt collar around the neck.

1. Make two pom-poms

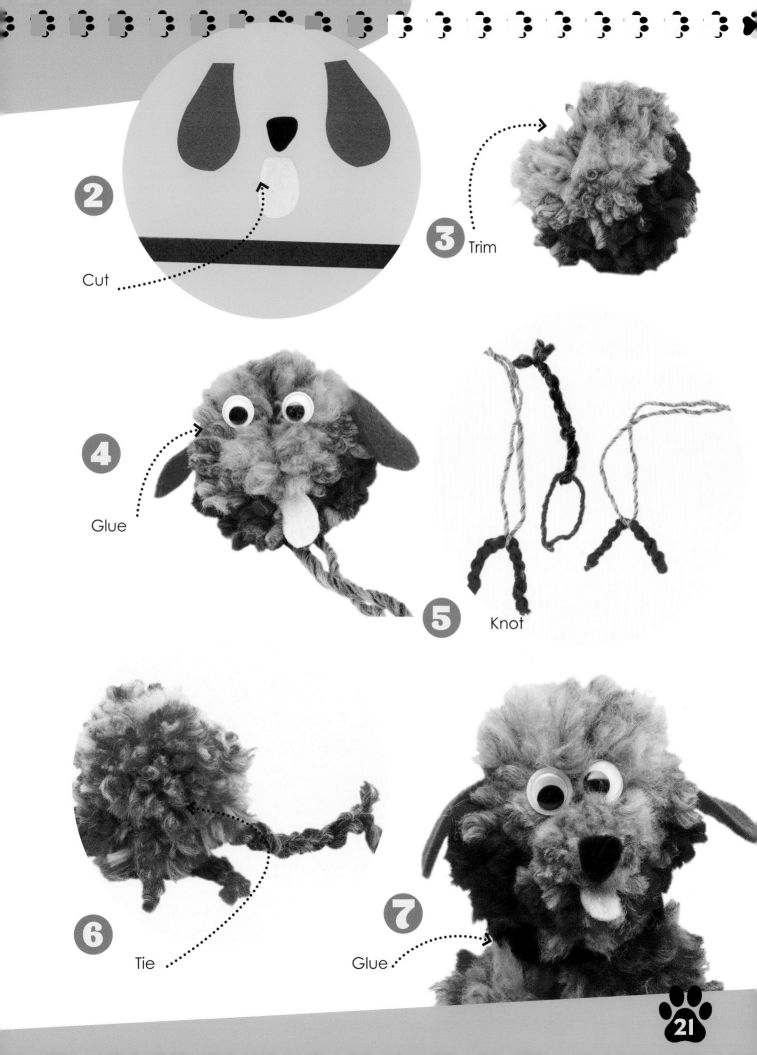

2

Cut

3 Trim

4

Glue

5 Knot

6

Tie

7

Glue

fleece Rope

Make fleece ropes for your dog to play with. Dogs love to play tug-of-war with ropes.

Tools & Materials:

- ✔ Fleece fabric (can be new or reused from an old blanket or sweater)
- ✔ Scissors
- ✔ Ruler

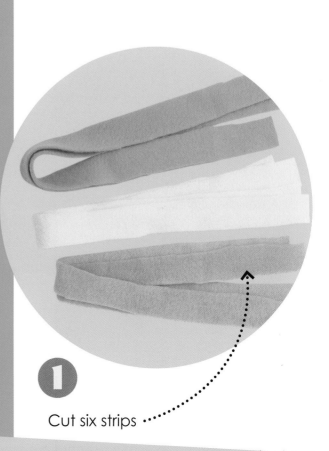

1. Cut six strips of fleece about 2 inches (5 cm) wide. It is not important that they be exactly the same width. The length depends on how long you want the rope to be. The finished size is about a third of the length of the strip.

2. Lay your strips on top of each other in a pile.

3. Make a knot at one end.

4. Have someone hold the knotted end or tape it to a board or table. It needs to be **stationary** while you pull on the fleece. Seperate the fleece into three pairs of two strands each. Begin braiding the fleece.

5. As you braid, tug the braid gently after each pass.

6. When you get near the end, make another knot and pull tightly.

1

Cut six strips

Another IDEA!
Make the rope using wider strips of fleece. It will make a thicker rope.

2 Make a pile

3 Knot

4 Secure

Braid

6 Knot

Toy Box

Dogs love toys. Make them a toy box to store all their toys. With a lot of patience you can train them to put their own toys away.

Tools & Materials:

- ✔ Cardboard box (if your dog chews cardboard boxes use a plastic bin)
- ✔ Paint and brush
- ✔ Images (photos, stickers, or cloth such as old pajamas)
- ✔ Paper-mache glue
- ✔ Corrugated cardboard
- ✔ Scissors

1. Find a box that would be a good size for your dog's toys. If it has flaps, have an adult cut them off.

2. Paint the outside of the box.

3. Paint the inside of the box.

4. Cut out images to decorate the box.

5. Brush glue on the back of the image. Place it on the box. Smooth it out. Continue with more pieces until you are pleased with the look of the box. Add stickers or words cut from a dog magazine.

6. Use the pattern on page 30 to cut out a bone-shaped piece of cardboard. On a piece of white paper or cardboard, write your dog's name and the word "toys." Glue the white paper to the cardboard bone.

7. Glue the cardboard bone to the box.

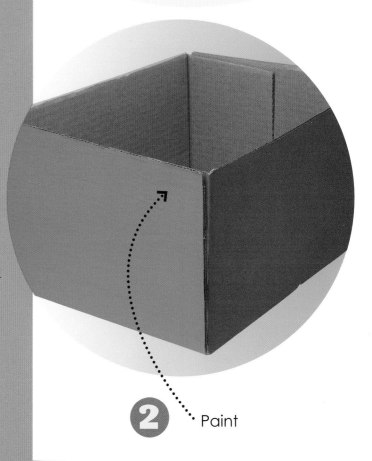

2 ····· Paint

3 Paint

4 Cut images

5 Glue

6 Glue

Toby's Toys

Add stickers

WOOF

7 Glue

woof

good dog

WOOF

Toby's Toys

25

Crazy Ball

Make a crazy ball with a tennis ball and fleece strips. You can throw it or play tug-of-war with the fleece extensions.

Tools & Materials:

✔ Fleece (can be an old scarf, sweater, or pajamas)
✔ Scissors and ruler
✔ Tennis ball

1. Cut strips of fleece. Make two of them 2 inches (5 cm) wide × 24 inches (61 cm) long. Cut seven other strips about 1 inch (3 cm) wide. (It's not important that they all be the same width.) Cut one short strip about 6 inches (15 cm) long.

2. Make a cross shape with the two wider strips. Place the tennis ball in the center. Gather the strips around the ball and towards the center.

3. Tie the small strip around the gathered strips. Tie it as close to the tennis ball as you can. Pull the strips covering the tennis ball tight. Wrap the strip around the gathering again and make a knot.

4. Start weaving the other strips through the strips tied to the ball. Weave each strip around the ball once, leaving two long ends. Continue weaving new strips until the ball is covered.

5. Tie each pair of strips together using an overhand knot. Continue making knots until you have 1 to 2 inches (3–5 cm) of strip left. If the remaing strip is uneven, cut the extra part off. Cut fringes in the fleece ends.

1. Cut fleece strips

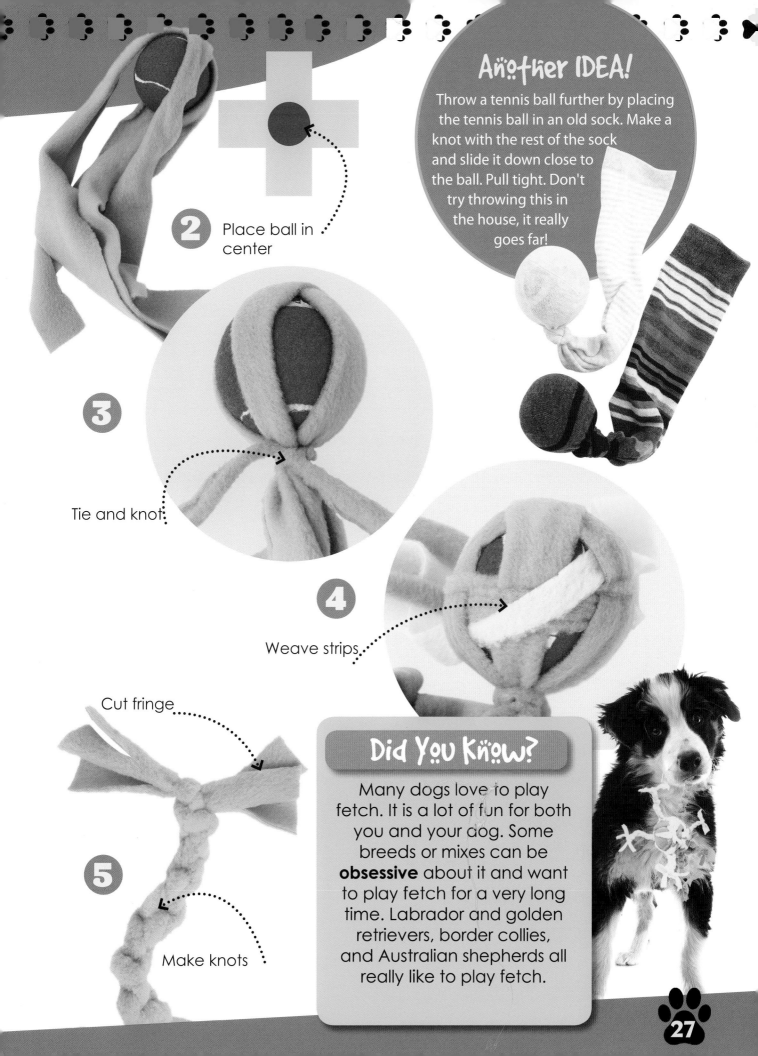

2 Place ball in center

3 Tie and knot

4 Weave strips

5 Cut fringe

Make knots

Another IDEA!

Throw a tennis ball further by placing the tennis ball in an old sock. Make a knot with the rest of the sock and slide it down close to the ball. Pull tight. Don't try throwing this in the house, it really goes far!

Did You Know?

Many dogs love to play fetch. It is a lot of fun for both you and your dog. Some breeds or mixes can be **obsessive** about it and want to play fetch for a very long time. Labrador and golden retrievers, border collies, and Australian shepherds all really like to play fetch.

fancy collar

Dress your dog up with a fancy dress collar.

Tools & Materials:

✔ Dress shirt with collar
✔ Scissors
✔ Fabric paint
✔ Glue
✔ Sequins

❶ Find a dress shirt with a collar. (A thrift store is a good place to find one.) Use your dog's collar as a guide for sizing.

❷ Lay the shirt out flat. Use scissors to cut the collar away from the shirt. Cut as close to the **seam** as you can.

❸ Decorate the edge of the collar with fabric paint.

❹ Glue sequins to the collar.

❶

Select shirt

❷

Cut

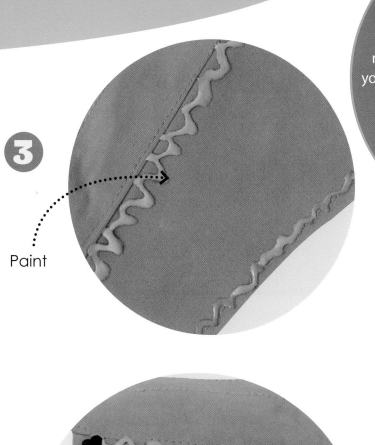

3

Paint

Another IDEA!

Decorate the collar with buttons rather than paint and sequins. Maybe your dog would prefer fake jewels. Make a bejeweled collar.

Did You Know?

Dogs usually have tags attached to their collars that have their name and owner's contact info and show they have their rabies vaccine. Some dogs also have a microchip implanted in their skin. This tiny chip can be scanned to identify a lost dog even if its collar and tags are missing.

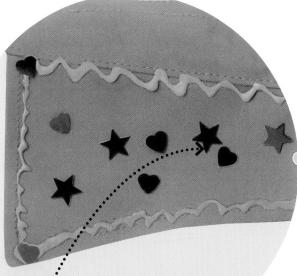

4

Glue

TIP

Place this collar over your dog's regular collar with the ID tags on it.

29

Patterns

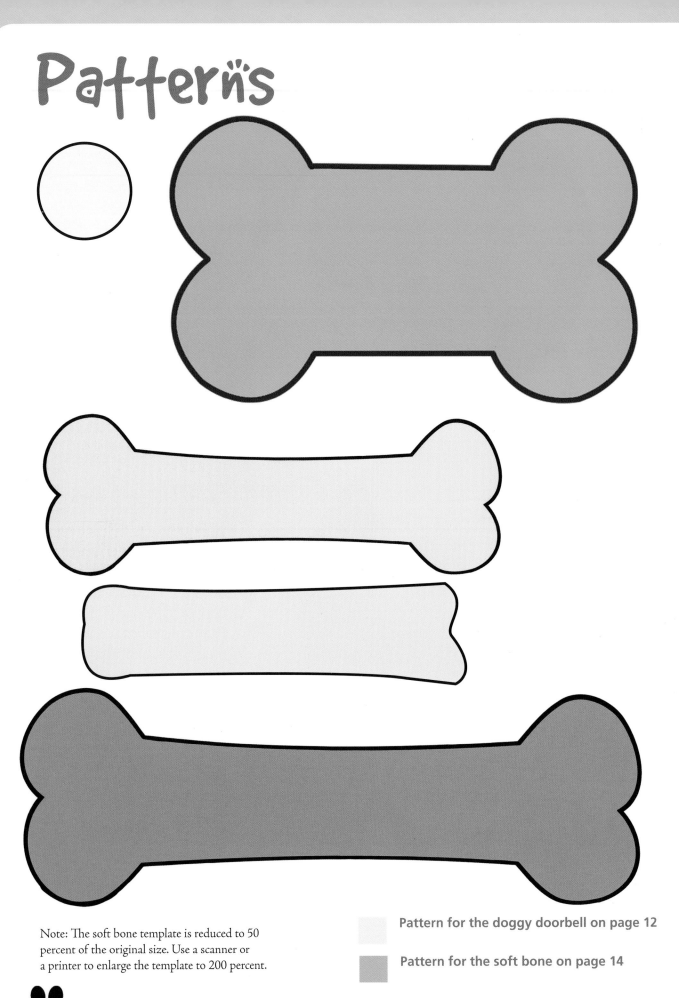

Note: The soft bone template is reduced to 50 percent of the original size. Use a scanner or a printer to enlarge the template to 200 percent.

Pattern for the doggy doorbell on page 12

Pattern for the soft bone on page 14

MAKING POM-POMS

❯ Using the pattern below, cut out two cardboard circle shapes. Place them together.

❯ Take a long strand of bulky yarn and start winding it around the circle. Wind a thick layer. The more yarn, the thicker the pom-pom. If you run out of yarn, just start winding a new strand.

❯ Place scissors between the two cardboard circles and cut the yarn. Cut a piece of yarn and wind it between the two cardboard circles. Pull the yarn tight and make a double knot. Remove the cardboard.

❯ Trim the pom-pom so it is even.

Wind around the cardboard.

Cut

Tie

Pattern for the dog frame on page 18

Pattern for the pom-pom puppy on page 20

Pattern for the toy box on page 24

Glossary

obsessive Extremely concerned about or devoted to something.

right side The printed or top side of fabric.

seam A way to join layers of fabric together with a line of stitches.

stationary Not moving.

tapestry A heavy cloth that has designs or pictures woven into it.

template Pattern.

For More Information

Further Reading

Sundance, Kyra. *101 Dog Tricks, Kids Edition: Fun and Easy Activities, Games, and Crafts.* Beverly, MA: Quarry Books, 2014.

Thomas, Isabel. *Designer Dog Projects.* Chicago, IL: Heinemann Raintree, 2016.

Websites

Dogs
www.ducksters.com/animals/dogs.php
Find out more about these great pets here!

Domestic Dogs
www.dkfindout.com/us/animals-and-nature/dogs/domestic-dogs/
This page has information on many different dog breeds.

Index